SONGS TO SHARE

מַתְּנַת שִׁיר

מַתְּנַת שִׁיר

Songs to Share

by ROSE B. GOLDSTEIN

Piano settings by REUVEN KOSAKOFF

Illustrated by E. SCHLOSS

5710   1949

NEW YORK

The United Synagogue Commission on Jewish Education

לבחורי

בחירי לבי

ממני

„אם הבנים שמחה"

TO MY BOYS

David Aaron
Jonathan Amos
Jeremy Eliezer
Alexander Menaḥem
Nason Samuel

PREFACE

THE EXTENT to which Jewish religious values are caught and held in song needs no demonstration to anyone who has experienced the full-bodied Jewish tradition of worship and study. Religious Jews have always found support in song. They chanted their prayers, sang their *Zemirot*, and intoned their studies.

These little songs are aimed at leading American Jewish children into happy participation in religious living. They grew out of my own attempt to meet the needs of my youngest son, Nason Samuel. In words and music, simple enough even for the pre-school child, they lay a basis for the establishment of fundamental attitudes and habits characteristic of traditional Judaism. Mothers in the home and teachers in the classroom will surely find these songs useful. But their appeal is not limited to small children. All but a few are suitable for general use.

A number of the melodies are of my own composition. Other texts are set to familiar synagogue tunes which the child will recognize with pleasure when he begins to attend the synagogue service. "Pesaḥ, Season of Cheer" (*Ki Lo Na-eh*), handed down in my family for generations, from Great-grandfather Tevye Schatz, to Grandmother Libby Cohen, to Mother Sarah Rachel Berman (ז״ל), is a melody which I have never seen in print.

The piano settings by Reuven Kosakoff are more than accompaniments. They are in themselves an artistic achievement which materially enhances the value of the book. Thus arranged, these songs may be offered for public performance without apology.

To Cantor Aaron I. Edgar of Omaha, Nebraska, who formed my taste for synagogue music, I owe a debt of gratitude. Thanks are also due to the Readers of the Music Committee of the United Synagogue Commission on Jewish Education for reading the manuscript, and to Rabbi Abraham E. Millgram who has been most generous and helpful in seeing the book through to publication. To my good friends, Julietta K. Arthur, Eric Mandell, Rabbi and Mrs. Simon Greenberg, and, above all, to my dear husband, Rabbi David A. Goldstein, my appreciation for the sustained encouragement which enabled me to complete this project.

ROSE B. GOLDSTEIN

CONTENTS

PART ONE

Songs for Every Day

Slowly, with majesty

Mo - deh.... a - ni l'-fa - ne - ḥa   Me - leḥ ḥai v'-ka - yam She-he-he-

Modeh Ani

zar-ta bi nish-ma - ti b'-ḥem-lah....... Ra - bah....... e - mu-na - te - ḥa.

give thanks unto Thee,
living and eternal King,
Who hast restored my soul unto me in mercy:
reat is Thy faithfulness.

מוֹדֶה אֲנִי לְפָנֶיךָ,
מֶלֶךְ חַי וְקַיָּם,
שֶׁהֶחֱזַרְתָּ בִּי נִשְׁמָתִי בְּחֶמְלָה,
רַבָּה אֱמוּנָתֶךָ.

Happily

Thank You for the sun,.......... Big and round and bright;..........

These lyrics are based on the Yotzer Or *blessing from the* Shaḥar

Good Morning

Thank You dear lov-ing God, For the morn-ing light....... Thank You for my-self,..........

Grow-ing straight and strong; Thank You for list-'ning, God, To my hap-py song!

III

Resolutely   *Traditional*

Ba — ruḥ   at — tah a — do — nai   E — lo — hey — nu me-leḥ ha-o-

We   bless   You, Lord, our   God,   Dear   Fa — ther of   us

Grace Before Meals

lam,.......... Ha - mo - tzi le - hem min ha - a - retz.....
all, ... *Whose* *earth* *gives* *food* *to* .... *great* *and* *small*.....

בָּרוּךְ אַתָּה אֲדֹנָי
אֱלֹהֵינוּ מֶלֶךְ הָעוֹלָם,
הַמּוֹצִיא לֶחֶם מִן הָאָרֶץ.

15

IV

Fast, playfully

Mag-dil y'shu-ot Mal — — ko V'— o — seh he-sed li-me-shi — ho

Thank You, our dear Fa — — — ther........ Thank You for the food we eat;

Grace After Meals

L'do - vid ul - zar - o......... ad o - lam.... sweet.
Thank You for our pa-rents, Who make life so

cresc.

מַגְדִּיל יְשׁוּעוֹת מַלְכּוֹ
וְעֹשֶׂה חֶסֶד לִמְשִׁיחוֹ,
לְדָוִד וּלְזַרְעוֹ עַד עוֹלָם.

The Hebrew text, Psalm 18, 51, is sung at the end of the traditional Grace After Meals.
The English lyrics are based on the general theme of the Grace After Meals.

Welcome Song

Your bright face makes us glad to-day,...... God bless us all !...........
Ev'-ry day grate-ful chil-dren say,...... "God bless us all !"...........

cresc.

To take notice of the return of a child after absence.

19

March tempo, heroic

Have we not one Fa — — — ther? All men are bro — thers.
One law for the home — — born; All men are bro — thers.

Bible Sources: Malachi 2, 10; Exodus 12, 49.

All Men Are Brothers

Black and white He loves a - like; All men are bro - thers.....
Same law for the stran - - - - ger; All men are bro - thers.....

Counter melody from Beethoven's 9th Symphony

Moderately, merrily

Solo

I have some fine new shoes; My mom-my bought for
I have a big red ball; My dad-dy gave to

p   sempre stacc.

Song for New Things

me! wear them in the best of health, You're lu-cky as can be!....
me! Use it in the best of health, You're lu-cky as can be!....

rog Gezunterheit" *and* "Nutz Gezunterheit" *are sentiments too precious for children to abandon even if they do not know Yiddish.*

Moderately, serious mood

1. Some-thing to spend, and some-thing to share, Yes, that's what mo-ney is for!......
2. Sab-bath's our hol-i day, comes ev'-ry week, Yes, Sab-bath's the day I love best......

24

Something to Share

1. Since I am lit-tle, I've lit - tle to give, But when I grow big, I'll give more! .....
2. Not un-til mo-ney is dropped in the box, May Sab-bath can-dles be blest. ....

f

dim.

pp

1 2 1 2 1
            3

2
4

Slowly lullaby

1. Blest art Thou, O Lord, our God, Who makes the night to fall; Thou
2. *Bless my bed and bless my head!...... Teach me of Thy ways!*

Evensong

1. send—est sleep to tir — ed eyes And bring-est rest to all.....
2. When I sleep and when I wake, I'll thank Thee all my days....

The words are based on the traditional Hebrew prayer (Hamapil) which is recited upon retiring at night.

Slowly, prayer

1. Ba-ruh a-do-nai ba-yom, Ba-ruh a-do-nai.... ba-lai-lah, Ba-

2. *Blest art Thou, God, by day! Blest art Thou, Lord, when the light is done!*

God Is Always With Us

1. ruḥ a-do-nai b'shoḥ-bey-nu,.... Ba-ruḥ a-do-nai b'ku-mey-nu........
2. Blest art Thou nights when we slum-ber;........ Blest when the.... new day's be-gun.............

בָּרוּךְ אֲדֹנָי בַּיּוֹם,
בָּרוּךְ אֲדֹנָי בַּלַּיְלָה,
בָּרוּךְ אֲדֹנָי בְּשָׁכְבֵנוּ,
בָּרוּךְ אֲדֹנָי בְּקוּמֵנוּ.

To be chanted after the Shema both morning and evening.

Slowly, with great feeling

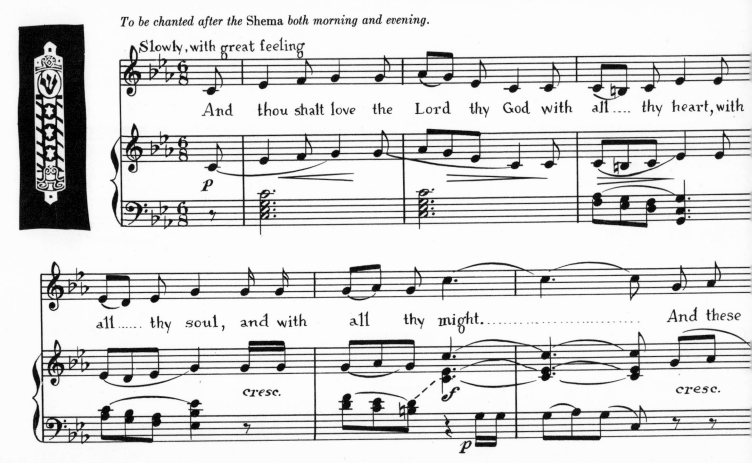

And thou shalt love the Lord thy God with all.... thy heart, with all...... thy soul, and with all thy might.................... And these

And Thou Shalt Love

words which I com - mand thee this day shall be up - on thy

heart. And thou shalt teach them di-li-gent-ly un-to thy child-ren, And shalt

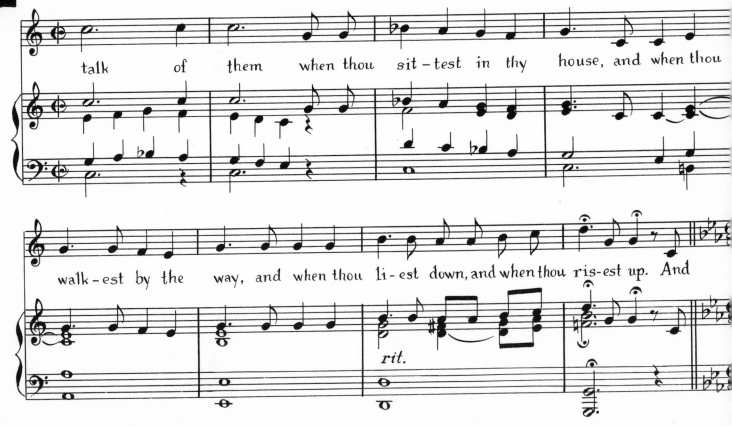

talk of them when thou sit‑test in thy house, and when thou walk‑est by the way, and when thou li‑est down, and when thou ris‑est up. And

rit.

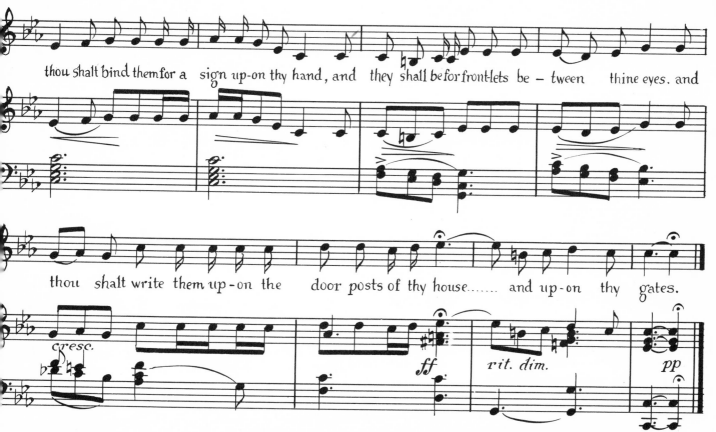

thou shalt bind them for a sign up-on thy hand, and they shall be for front-lets be — tween thine eyes. and

thou shalt write them up-on the door posts of thy house....... and up-on thy gates.

cresc.

ff

rit. dim.

pp

Very slow

Hi-ney lo ya-num v' – lo yi – – shan   sho-mer   sho-mer   Yis-ra-el.
He will not slum-ber,   He will not sleep,   God o-ver Is-ra-el His   watch does keep.

ה לֹא יָנוּם וְלֹא יִישָׁן
שׁוֹמֵר יִשְׂרָאֵל.

Psalm 121, 4.

34

PART TWO

Songs for Round the Year

The Jewish Year

Ni - san, I - yar, Si - van....... The sum - mer has be - gun, Tam -

muz, Av and E - lul,....... Va - ca - tion days, then school.

D. C. AL FINE

Sabbath Song

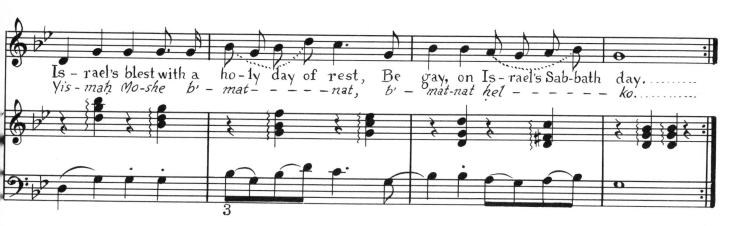

Is - rael's blest with a ho - ly day of rest, Be gay, on Is - rael's Sab - bath day.

Yis - maḥ Mo-she b' - mat - - - - - nat, b' - mat-nat hel - - - - - - ko.

XV

Slowly, with majesty

Traditional

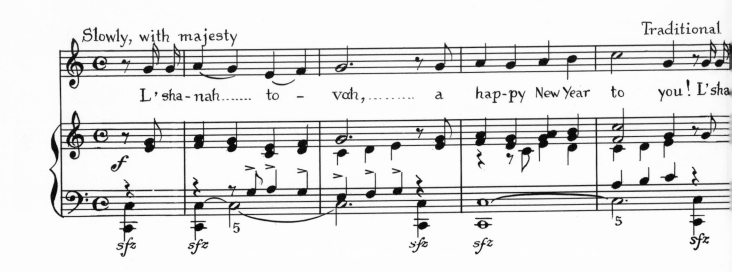

L' sha-nah....... to - vah,......... a hap-py New Year to you! L'sha

לְשָׁנָה טוֹבָה תִּכָּתֵבוּ.

A Happy New Year

nah to- vah   ti -ka -tey .— vu,   The   same   to   you!

Slowly, sadly

Traditional

Each pray-ing Jew....... be-gins a — new....... All the
V' - al .... ku - - lam............... E - lo-

וְעַל כֻּלָם אֱלוֹהַ סְלִיחוֹת,
סְלַח לָנוּ, מְחַל לָנוּ, כַּפֶּר לָנוּ.

Yom Kippur Day

March, with inspiration

Traditional

Ho - sha nah! .... we ce - le - brate Suk - kot, Ho - sha
Ho - sha nah! .... ho - - - - sha nah! L'mar

f

הוֹשַׁע נָא, הוֹשַׁע נָא,
לְמַעַנְךָ אֱלֹהֵינוּ,
הוֹשַׁע נָא, הוֹשַׁע נָא.

"Hosha Na" may be translated, "O God, please help us!" It is used in the synagogue during the march with Lulav and Etrog

44

For Sukkot

nah! .... with Et-rog and Lu-lav. .... Har-vest fruits hang from the Suk-kah's
ha .... E-lo - - - hey nu, ... ho - - - - - - sha

walls, ... Through the boughs we see the stars a-bove. ....
nah! .... Ho - - - - - - - - sha nah! ....

XVIII

Gaily

Hasidic

1. Ab - ram danced on
2. Ja - cob sang on
3. Sa - rah danced on
4. Le - ah sang on

Sim-ḥat To - rah On Sim-ḥat, Sim-ḥat To - rah.

For Simhat Torah

1. I - saac laughed on
2. Mo - ses clapped on
3. Riv - ka laughed on
4. Ra - chel clapped on

Sim-hat To - rah On Sim-hat To - - rah..........

p cresc.

dim.

p

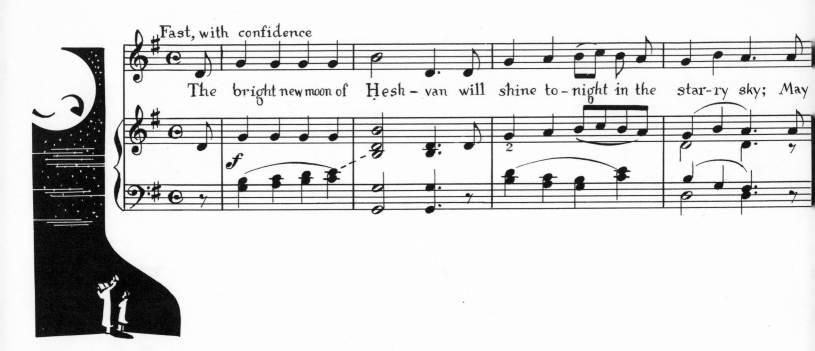

The bright new moon of Hesh — van will shine to-night in the star-ry sky; May

New Moon

life and peace and health and joy Bless us from on... high....... A - men.

Moderately, spirited

1. Au-tumn leaves are fall-ing down, Gold-en yel-low, red and brown, Float-ing to the
2. Rosh Ha-sha-nah came and went, Suk-kot week in joy was spent Work-ing days are

Autumn Song

ground here! With a rustl-ing sound.

Fill a fruit-ful year.

Slowly, proudly

A 3-Voice Round

Who's the he — ro of the sto — ry! How the Jews were

Who's the Hero? [For Ḥanukah—A 3-Voice Round]

crowned with glo — ry?   Mac - ca - be - us,   Mac - ca - be - us!

Who's the mad king in the story,
How the Jews were crowned with glory?
Antiochus, Antiochus.

How do we recall the story,
How the Jews were crowned with glory?
Candles tell us. Candles tell us.

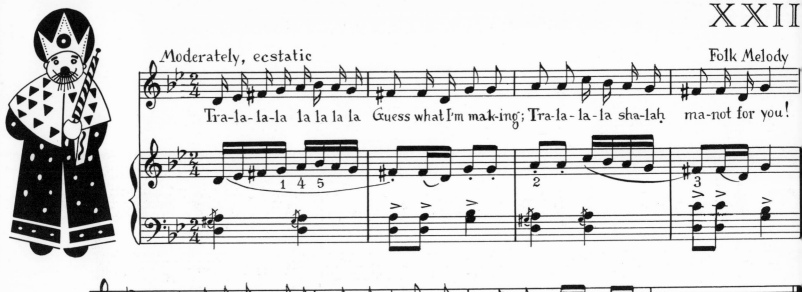

Purim Time Is Fun

Read the old Me - gil - lah scroll, Thanks to Es - ther and to Mor - de - cai,

We are here to play our role Pass-ing all the wick-ed Ha-mans by!..........

Laugh for glad-ness ha, ha, ha! Cheer our he - roes, Rah, rah, rah!

Tra- la la, sing all as one......... Pu-rim time is.... fun!

D.C. AL FINE

The melody is based on the Yiddish folk song דער רבי האט געהייסען פרייליך זיין. The words may be difficult for small children to master. Use solo voice and have the group join as indicated.

56

XXIII   Pesah, Season of Cheer

Melody handed down in family of R. B. G.

With great hilarity

Pe-sah sea-son of cheer,............ Spring time of the year,............
Ki lo na — — — eh,............ ki lo ya — — eh,............

Wel - come dear-est of feast days! Pass-o-ver se-der's here........
Ad - dir bim lu - - ḥah............ Ba - ḥur ka-ha-la - ḥah,........

God set our peo-ple free, Led them safe a - cross the sea,......
G'du - dav.... yom-ru lo l' - - ḥa........... u - l' - ḥa,......

gradually faster and louder

Put an end to slav - er - y, Did it all for you and me.
l' - ha..... ki l' ha l' - ha.......... af l' ha l'-

gradually slow down to first speed

Praise..... the Lord in song and psalm! Bam ti-ri, bam ti-ri, bam bam bam,
ha a-do-nai ha-mam-la-hah, Bam ti-ri, bam ti-ri, bam bam bam.

Pe - sah sea-son of cheer,........... Spring time of the year!

Ki lo na - - - eh .... *ki lo ya - - - eh!*

כִּי לוֹ נָאֶה, כִּי לוֹ יָאֶה:
אַדִּיר בִּמְלוּכָה,
בָּחוּר כַּהֲלָכָה.
גְּדוּדָיו יֹאמְרוּ לוֹ,
לְךָ וּלְךָ, לְךָ כִּי לְךָ,
לְךָ אַף לְךָ,
לְךָ אֲדֹנָי הַמַּמְלָכָה,
כִּי לוֹ נָאֶה, כִּי לוֹ יָאֶה.

With pride

Ha - yom yom hu - la - d' - ti............ Hey - dad! hey-dad! hey-
I'm five....... years old to - day,........ Hur - rah! hur-rah! hur-

dad! .... G'do — lah hi sim — ḥa — ti .... Nir — ko — dah yad b'-
ray! .... In Ju — dy's hon-or all say .... "Man — y hap-py re- turns of the

yad. La la la la la la .... La la la la la
day."

merrily

la........... Ha - yom yom hu - la - d' - ti........ Hey - dad! hey-dad! hey-dad!

I'm five..... years old to - day........ Hur - rah! hur-rah! hur-ray!

הַיוֹם יוֹם הֻלַּדְתִּי,
הֵידָד, הֵידָד, הֵידָד.
גְּדוֹלָה הִיא שִׂמְחָתִי,
נִרְקוֹדָה יָד בְּיָד.

הַיוֹם יוֹם הֻלַּדְתְּךָ ...

UNITED SYNAGOGUE COMMISSION ON JEWISH EDUCATION

Azriel Eisenberg, *Chairman*   Leo L. Honor, *Vice-Chairman*   Josiah Derby, *Secretary*

Eli Bohnen	Henry R. Goldberg	A. Hillel Henkin	Judah Pilch
Ben Bokser	Morris S. Goodblatt	Ario S. Hyams	Louis L. Ruffman
Elias Charry	Jacob B. Grossman	Alter F. Landesman	Zevi Scharfstein
Moshe Davis	Peretz Halpern	Harry O. H. Levine	Samuel Sussman

EX OFFICIO

Albert I. Gordon, *Executive Director, United Synagogue of America*

Abraham E. Millgram, *Educational Director, United Synagogue of America*

Simon Greenberg, *Provost, Jewish Theological Seminary of America*

Max J. Routtenberg, *Executive Vice-President, Rabbinical Assembly of America*

COMMITTEE ON MUSIC

Ario S. Hyams, *Chairman*

Harry Coopersmith	David Putterman
Judith Eisenstein	Edward T. Sandrow
Abraham E. Millgram	Robert Segal